KU-724-589

THIS BOOK BELONGS TO

....

....

....

FOR JOHN "CRISPS" ENGLISH, WHO BROUGHT GROG TO LIFE
S.K.

First published 2017 by Walker Books Ltd, 87 Vauxhall Walk,
London SE11 5HJ
in association with Historic Royal Palaces, Hampton Court Palace,
Surrey KT8 9AU
2 4 6 8 10 9 7 5 3 1
Text © 2017 Historic Royal Palaces
Illustrations © 2017 Walker Books Ltd and Historic Royal Palaces
Illustrations by Peter Cottrill
This book has been set in Goudy, WPG Amatic SC
Printed in Turkey

All rights reserved. No part of this book may be reproduced,
transmitted or stored in an information retrieval system in any
form or by any means, graphic, electronic or mechanical, including
photocopying, taping and recording, without prior written permission
from the publisher.

British Library Cataloguing in Publication Data: a catalogue record
for this book is available from the British Library
ISBN 978-1-4063-7688-3
www.walker.co.uk
www.hrp.org.uk

**WALKER
BOOKS**

TERRIBLE
TRUE TALES FROM THE
TOWER OF LONDON

SARAH KILBY   ILLUSTRATED BY **PETER COTTRILL**

CONTENTS

FIND THE
ANSWERS TO THE
QUIZZES ON PAGES
124–125

INTRODUCTION

Find out about the ravens at the Tower of London.

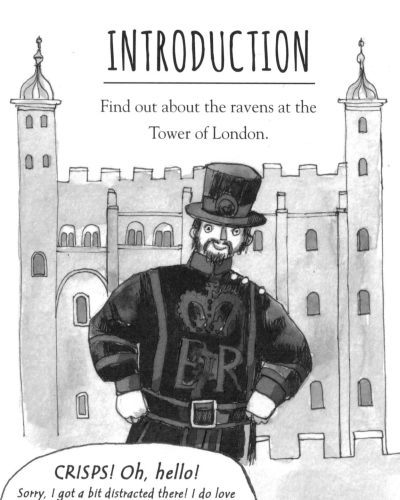

CRISPS! *Oh, hello!*
Sorry, I got a bit distracted there! I do love a salty snack. My name is Grog. I'm one of the seven ravens who live at the Tower of London. It's a pleasure to meet you.
In this book we ravens are going to tell you some true and terrible tales from the Tower's history. These are the stories some people would rather were kept secret! But first, let me tell you a little bit about the ravens and what we do here at the Tower.

HISTORY OF THE TOWER OF LONDON

It's our job to look after the Tower of London and I tell you, it's a very important job indeed. I know the Yeoman Warders in their fancy uniforms look like they are the Tower's guards, but as you will discover, they can't always be relied on to do the job properly!

The reason ravens live at the Tower of London is because of an ancient legend. It says that if we ever leave here, both the Tower and the kingdom will fall. So today, there are always seven of us living inside the Tower walls. Six of us are on duty and one of us is in reserve – just in case of mishaps. We are looked after by a Yeoman Warder known as the Ravenmaster. It's a bit of an odd name, because actually he's not really our master at all. We love bossing him around!

We keep the Yeoman Warders on their toes, by patrolling the massive stone fortress on the banks of the River Thames. The Tower dates to the 1070s and we guard its ancient treasures, such as the priceless Crown Jewels, which are still used to crown the kings and queens of Britain.

ROYAL RESPECT

There have always been ravens at the Tower of London. Don't let anyone tell you that we've only been here since Victorian times – I like to think I can trace my ancestry back to the Roman times when Emperor Claudius (10 BC – AD 54) founded the ancient settlement of Londinium. But by all accounts, life in the olden days was much wilder and far less comfortable. Then the Tower ravens lived in trees and scavenged food scraps from the kitchens. Only when Charles II

(1660–1685) was on the throne did we start to be treated with
the respect we deserved, although there was a bit of a to-do
here along the way.

According to the old stories,
passed down from beak to beak,
the problem started when John
Flamsteed, the first Astronomer Royal,
set up a telescope on the roof of the
White Tower so he could study the
moon in 1674. Ravens are naturally
curious birds and there may have
been, ahem, a few unfortunate
incidents involving the Tower's wild
ravens and broken glass in Flamsteed's telescope.

I'M GETTING THE BIRD'S-EYE VIEW!

Flamsteed was furious when he discovered his broken telescope
and demanded that the birds were removed from the Tower. But
luckily Charles II remembered the legend and refused. It is said
(although it might just be another story) that he issued a royal
decree protecting us for ever. Flamsteed had to find a new place
for his stargazing, and was given his own Royal Observatory at
Greenwich instead. We have been here at the Tower ever since,
keeping a beady eye
on things.

RAVEN RESIDENCE

In return for helping to protect the Tower and the kingdom over the years, we are now very well looked after by the Yeoman Warders. In fact, the Ravenmaster's job is to tend to our every need. We live in luxurious lodgings, called aviaries, inside the Tower's walls and eat tasty food. The Ravenmaster feeds us 170 grams of raw meat and delicious blood-soaked bird-biscuits every day, plus as many snacks as we can pinch from you visitors!

There are a few downsides to life at the Tower, of course. While we're partial to your packed lunches, the visitors can be rather annoying. You clutter up the place for one thing. We do our official photocall once a day, but you never seem to know when to stop pointing those cameras and telephones at us. It gets right up my beak, but some of the others secretly love the selfies. But we know you enjoy seeing us so we don't mind putting up with you – just don't try and stroke us!

RAVEN RESEARCH

We always hear the Yeoman Warders telling visitors the same old stories about what happened within these walls. Now don't get me wrong – those tales *are* interesting. But there are some things that the official guides don't tell you about the Tower. And we've decided it's time to reveal these UNOFFICIAL tales, which are full of mishaps and mayhem. It's a bit naughty of us to do this, so please don't tell the Yeoman Warders!

When we're in a group, you call us an "unkindness of ravens", which might not be as menacing as a "murder of crows" but is still a bit, well, unkind. We would *never* say such rude things about the Yeoman Warders or the Ravenmaster. But there's not a lot that escapes the notice of a Tower raven. We've got stories of terror, torture and some very silly human behaviour – and they are all true! These have become the stuff of raven legend and many have been passed down by raven relatives who saw history happening right in front of their beady eyes. You won't believe some of the things they've seen!

TURN OVER TO
MEET THE GANG!

THE RAVENS OF THE TOWER

I'm Grog, and I'm top of the pecking order. I can trace my ancestry back to the Romans. I like to think I always look on the bright side of life, and my one great love is that salty potato snack you humans call crisps!

Each one of the gang is going to tell you some of their favourite stories about life at the Tower. Let me introduce them:

HARRIS

A bit of a bruiser and a gangster, who's seen it all before, this bird loves a bit of guts and gore. Harris (or 'Arris as he calls himself) comes from a rough old family of East End ravens who've been hanging around the Tower for years.

CORA

All ravens like bright objects but Cora is a big fan of glamour and loves shiny things. If you ask me, she's a bit of a drama queen. She adores the Crown Jewels and thinks she's the Tower's expert on them.

GRIPP

Mr G is our clown and mischief-maker, a relentless buffoon and a practical joker. He's been known to lie on his back and play dead, which terrifies the tourists but fails to impress the Ravenmaster.

Edgar's a crusty but kindly old soldier who's served at the Tower with distinction. He likes things done properly: it's his job to whip the new recruits into shape. Some of the younger ravens are rather scared of him but he always has a twinkle in his eye.

EDGAR

MUNIN

Munin's a hippy chick, a bit of a wild thing, rather away with the fairies, truth be told. She's known as the flighty one – but she can tell you why!

HECTOR

Hector was nearly sacked for attacking the Governor's wife at a Tower party (he claims he thought her new hat was an alien). He's a bit unpredictable and he's a have-a-go hero, like his great-uncle Bert, who flew to the aid of the Tower's zookeeper (allegedly).

KINGS AND QUEENS OF BRITAIN

HOUSE OF NORMANDY

WILLIAM I (The Conqueror)
1066–1087
WILLIAM II 1087–1100
HENRY I 1100–1135
STEPHEN 1135–1154

HOUSE OF PLANTAGENET

HENRY II 1154–1189
RICHARD I (The Lionheart) 1189–119
JOHN 1199–1216
HENRY III 1216–1272
EDWARD I 1272–1307
EDWARD II 1307–1327
EDWARD III 1327–1377
RICHARD II 1377–1399

HENRY VIII

HOUSE OF TUDOR

HENRY VII 1485–1509
HENRY VIII 1509–1547
EDWARD VI 1547–1553
MARY I 1553–1558
ELIZABETH I 1558–1603

HOUSE OF STUART

JAMES I 1603–1625
CHARLES I 1625–1649

HOUSE OF HANOVER

GEORGE I 1714–1727
GEORGE II 1727–1760
GEORGE III 1760–1820
GEORGE IV 1820–1830
WILLIAM IV 1830–1837
VICTORIA 1837–1901

VICTORIA

HENRY IV 1399–1413
HENRY V 1413–1422
HENRY VI 1422–1461
1470–1471
EDWARD IV 1461–1470
1471–1483
EDWARD V 1483
RICHARD III 1483–1485

RICHARD I (THE LIONHEART)

THE COMMONWEALTH
1649–1660

CHARLES II 1660–1685
JAMES II 1685–1688
WILLIAM III 1689–1702
and **MARY II** 1689–1694
ANNE 1702–1714*

*The first monarch of Great Britain

We know lots about the different kings and queens of Britain. Use this timeline to find out who ruled when.

HOUSE OF SAXE-COBURG-GOTHA

EDWARD VII 1901–1910

HOUSE OF WINDSOR

GEORGE V 1910–1936
EDWARD VIII 1936
GEORGE VI 1936–1952
ELIZABETH II succeeded 1952

ELIZABETH II

15

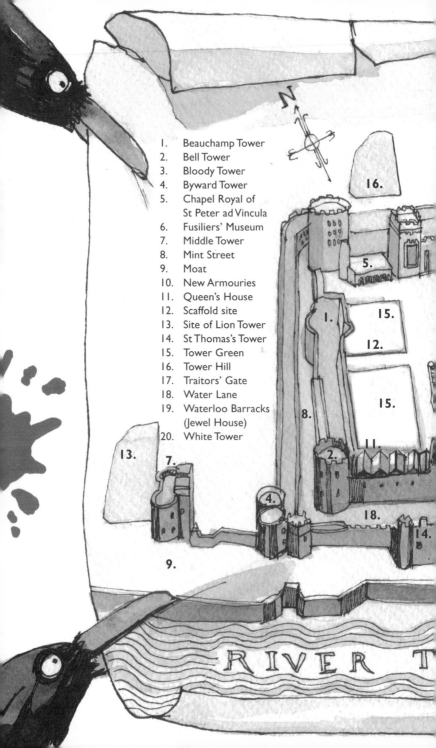

N

16.

5.

15.

12.

1.

15.

8.

11.

13.

7.

2.

4.

18.

14.

9.

RIVER T

BIRD'S-EYE VIEW OF THE TOWER

6.

20.

10.

MES

GROG'S GUIDE:
THE TOWER AT A GLANCE

1070: William the Conqueror starts to build the White Tower. It's finished in 1087 by his son William Rufus.

1216: Henry III becomes king and builds the first huge curtain wall around the White Tower.

1272: Edward I builds a second big wall encircling the fortress, and in 1279 sets up the largest mint in the country within the Tower walls.

1381: The Tower is invaded for the first and last time during the Peasants' Revolt.

1500s: The peak time for prisoners under the Tudors, with more people imprisoned and executed (including three queens) than at any other time.

1533: Henry VIII starts pimping the palace, including adding the onion domes, in preparation for the coronation of Anne Boleyn.

1590: The first (wealthy) paying visitors are shown around the Tower on guided tours.

1649: Following the Civil War, the Crown Jewels are destroyed: gems are sold off and gold crowns melted down in the Mint to make coins.

1661: The Crown Jewels are remade for the coronation of Charles II and then stored at the Tower ever afterwards.

1810: The Mint moves out to new secure premises on Tower Hill.

1830s: The last years of the Tower Menagerie. Most of the animals are moved to a new zoo in London's Regent's Park.

1901: Tourism swells – by the end of Queen Victoria's reign, over 500,000 people a year are visiting the Tower.

1940: During the Blitz, high explosives are dropped on the Tower and cause much damage. The White Tower narrowly escapes destruction.

2012: The Olympic torch is helicoptered into the Tower by a Royal Marine.

2017: The ravens become even more big-headed following the publication of *Terrible, True Tales from the Tower of London*.

CHAPTER ONE
HEADS OFF

Discover just how easy it was to lose your head at the Tower of London and the gruesome ways in which people were executed.

Did you know that ravens are often thought to be evil omens and symbols of death? Just because in days gone by we've hung around battlefields, pecking out the odd eyeball! But that was a long time ago – give me a nice crisp any day. Though it IS true that we love gory stories about the Tower. And who better to tell these tales than none other than our favourite East End villain?

So go ahead, HARRIS!

Now don't get me wrong, ladies and gents, I have a lot of respect for Grog, but some of us Tower ravens are made of tougher stuff – especially the East Enders. We've seen a few sights in our time, let me tell you. Here are my favourite stories of botched executions and grisly mistakes that'll make your blood run cold.

BEHEADING BUTCHERY

The Tower of London has been used as a place of execution for hundreds of years. The gents – and also ladies – who were executed here had all committed bigger crimes than nicking a bob or two. Most of them were high-born nobles who were guilty of treason, the crime of betraying your country. Regular traitors were normally hanged alive, disembowelled and cut into quarters. Or if they followed a different religion to everyone else, they were burnt alive while tied to a wooden stake.

Being beheaded at the Tower was seen as a far nicer way to die. With a sharp axe and a good aim, it was supposed to be quick and relatively painless. All the prisoner had to do was kneel blindfolded, with their neck on a wooden block, and it would be over before they knew it. In theory…

The trouble was that most English axemen were rubbish at their job. They were untrained and they weren't nice gents; they were bruisers who could start a fight in a tavern quicker than you could say, "Mine's a Bloody Mary." Many executioners were condemned criminals, who'd taken the dreaded job to escape their own death sentence. Add nerves, drunkenness and a blunt axe to the mix and beheadings were bound to get messy.

MISSED AGAIN!

GRISLY GREEN

Not many people – only seven in all – got their heads chopped off inside the Tower. You had to be really posh or even better, a really posh lady, to be beheaded in privacy on Tower Green.

Three queens were among the seven nobles who were executed by beheading on Tower Green. They were Anne Boleyn and Catherine Howard, the second and fifth wives of Henry VIII (1509–1547), who really got on his bad side, and Lady Jane Grey, who was queen for only nine days in 1553.

> *Bloody Mary was the nickname given to the Catholic Mary I (1553–1558) for her persecution of Protestants. During her reign around 300 people were executed by being burnt alive at the stake.*

Henry VIII had six wives. A handy way to remember what happened to each of them is to use this little rhyme:

KATHERINE OF ARAGON — DIVORCED

ANNE BOLEYN — BEHEADED

JANE SEYMOUR — DIED

ANNE OF CLEVES — DIVORCED

CATHERINE HOWARD — BEHEADED

KATERYN PARR — SURVIVED — YAY!

The other four were William Hastings, the Baron of Hastings, who was executed on the orders of Richard III (1483–1485); Margaret Pole, Countess of Salisbury, and Jane Boleyn, Viscountess Rochford, both executed on the orders of Henry VIII; and Robert Devereux, the Earl of Essex, executed on the orders of Elizabeth I (1558–1603). Today you can still see the place on Tower Green where these executions happened.

SWEET SWORD

Anne Boleyn requested an expert French swordsman, rather than an English axeman, for her execution on Tower Green in 1536 – and who can blame her? Her head was removed with one swift sword slice, so quickly, in fact, that the ravens who

A brain has enough oxygen to function for several seconds after it has been severed from the rest of the body, so reports of people's eyes and mouths moving after execution may be true.

were there said her eyes and mouth were still moving for a few seconds after death.

But Anne Boleyn was so certain that at the last minute Henry VIII would stop her execution and send her to a nunnery instead, that no one had organized a coffin. Her body had to be squashed into an old arrow box, with her head by her side. She was later buried in the Chapel Royal of St Peter ad Vincula at the Tower.

WHY DID HENRY VIII HAVE SO MANY WIVES? HE LIKED TO CHOP AND CHANGE!

HACKED OFF

Even worse was what happened to Margaret Pole, Countess of Salisbury, in 1541. Margaret made the dangerous choice to side with Henry VIII's first wife, Katherine of Aragon, over the king's divorce, and Henry had never forgiven her. He had the old lady imprisoned in a dirty, cold cell in the Tower between 1539 and 1541, before she was finally sentenced to death.

AND I THOUGHT I WAS AN OLD BIRD...

Margaret was nearly eighty by then, small and frail, but she was still proud. She had to be dragged onto Tower Green, where she then refused to kneel at the block. She was held down, and as she struggled, the panicking executioner struck a wild blow that gashed her shoulder. Despite her bleeding wound, the countess got up and tried to run away, but was chased around the block by the axe-wielding executioner. According to my great-grandmother, Ada, who loved a good gory tale, it took eleven blows to finish Margaret off, and her head and shoulders were hacked to pieces by the end.

BLIMEY, THOSE TUDORS WERE TERRIBLE!

ROYAL CHOPPING LIST

Robert Devereux, previously the Earl of Essex, was a favourite of Elizabeth I, but the queen went off him when she found out he was plotting to overthrow her. The handsome earl was sentenced to death for treason in 1601. Elizabeth tried to ensure that all went smoothly for her old pal and arranged to have two executioners on hand at the Tower, in case "one faints, the other may perform it". In the end, the axeman held his nerve, but still took three strikes to remove Devereux's head. He was the last person in history to be beheaded on Tower Green.

Walter Ralegh, an enemy of Robert Devereux, was one of the longest-serving prisoners at the Tower of London, spending thirteen years in the Bloody Tower. When he was finally beheaded in 1618, his grief-stricken widow had his head preserved, so she could keep it with her for the rest of her days.

OH WALT, YOU'RE QUIET TODAY!

DID YOU REMEMBER THE PICNIC?

HORRIBLE HILL

The rest of the traitorous riff-raff, who weren't posh enough for Tower Green, met a bloody end on Tower Hill, which is just a stone's throw away from here. Crowds of people would come to watch the executions, which were carried out on a big wooden platform (called a scaffold) so that everyone got a good view. Executions were very popular days out and people really enjoyed attending them. Over the years, many more people were executed on Tower Hill than on Tower Green – around one hundred.

BLOCK BRIBERY

Prisoners often gave money to their executioners, hoping for a quick and easy death. But executioners could also be bribed to make things worse for the prisoner. By the time Thomas Cromwell, once Henry VIII's chief minister, was sentenced to death in 1540, he had made many enemies. According to one story, Cromwell's hated rival, the Duke of Norfolk, was rumoured to have deliberately paid an inexperienced executioner to do the job – and then, for good measure, got the executioner drunk just before the beheading! The spectators who gathered around the scaffold on Tower Hill looked on in horror as the "ragged and boocherly myser" of an executioner hacked at Cromwell's head, taking at least three axe blows to finish him off. Cromwell's head was then stuck on a spike on London Bridge.

It was the executioner's job to parboil traitors' heads with cumin and salt before they were displayed on spikes on London Bridge. This supposedly kept the crows and ravens away.

I PREFER SALT AND VINEGAR!

KETCH-UP!

Given how unpopular executioners were, it's no surprise they usually kept their names a secret. However, one man, Jack Ketch, became so associated with the job that for years after, executioners were all known by the name of "Ketch". One of the first Ketchs made such a mess of beheading Lord Russell on Tower Hill in 1683 that the watching crowd booed him. Ketch was so offended that he published a pamphlet claiming that the bloodbath was not his fault, but Russell's for wriggling.

Two years later in 1685 it was the same Ketch's job to behead the young Duke of Monmouth on Tower Hill. Monmouth tipped Ketch six guineas, begging him, "Do not use me as you used poor Lord Russell." Little good it did him. Ketch lost his nerve, and shouted, "I can't do it!" His first blow gashed Monmouth's neck.

The second blow buried the axe in his shoulders. In all, it took "five Chopps" of the axe to sever his head from his body, and at the very end, Ketch had to use his butcher's knife to cut through the last strands of gristle.

LAST-LAUGH LOVAT

Lord Lovat, the Scottish leader of a group of rebellious nobles called the Jacobites, had the final laugh on the scaffold as he was the last man to be beheaded on Tower Hill in 1747 on the order of George II (1727–1760). Aged eighty, he faced his death cheerfully, comforting friends on the way to the block by saying, "Cheer up man, I'm not afraid, why should you be?" He remained calm – in complete contrast to the crowds of bloodthirsty spectators. The crush was so great that specially constructed stands around the scaffold collapsed, killing at least ten people. But the ten guineas he tipped the (unknown) executioner were well spent. He was executed cleanly, with one blow.

Eventually beheading went out of fashion (far too messy for most people). Instead the Tower was used to store jewels, money and weapons. The last person to be executed here was a German spy in World War II. He was shot by firing squad in 1941.

Although Lord Lovat was the last man to be beheaded on Tower Hill, beheading for treason was not formally abolished in English law until 1973.

HEADS OFF QUIZ

1. **Before being stuck on spikes, traitors' decapitated heads were parboiled with:**
   a) oil.
   b) cumin and salt.
   c) tomato juice and vinegar.
   d) alcohol.

2. **Elizabeth I hired two executioners to dispatch the Earl of Essex because:**
   a) she thought the Earl would run away.
   b) one executioner was new to the job.
   c) one might faint and the other could take over.
   d) the Earl had a very thick neck.

3. **What happened at the execution of Lord Russell in 1683?**
   a) The executioner cut off his own toe by mistake.
   b) The executioner was fined for time-wasting.
   c) Lord Russell refused to put his head on the block.
   d) The crowd booed the executioner for making such a mess.

4. **Which famous Thomas was imprisoned in the Tower by Henry VIII and later made a saint?**
   a) Thomas Cromwell
   b) Thomas More
   c) Thomas Becket
   d) Thomas the Tank Engine

5. **Why was Mary I known as "Bloody Mary"?**
   a) She liked drinking cocktails.
   b) She swore a lot.
   c) She had hundreds of Protestants burned at the stake.
   d) She suffered lots of nosebleeds.

CHAPTER TWO
CROWN JEWELS CALAMITIES

Find out about how the priceless Crown Jewels
have almost been lost and stolen.

Are the Crown Jewels real? Why does everyone ask that question?
Of COURSE they are! Would we really have huge metal doors and
reinforced glass cases for a collection of fakes? But I'll let Cora tell
you more. She loves diamonds, so she keeps a close eye on what
happens in the Jewel House – unless she's posing for a picture.
She'd nest on top of the Imperial State Crown if she could!

Darlings, old Groggie is right –
I love those jewels! But in the old
days some of your silly sovereigns
didn't treat them with the love
and care they deserve. I'm going
to tell you about some of the more
catastrophic calamities.

OLD? ME?
How dare you, Cora!

CROWNING GLORY

The Crown Jewels are a special collection of objects, kept at the Tower of London, which are used in the ceremony when a new king or queen is crowned. The Jewels are of such symbolic and sacred value that they are priceless. So you would think they would have been carefully looked after throughout history. But, I'm afraid to say, that hasn't always been the case and there have been one or two terrible calamities and near

DARLINGS, THANK GOODNESS I'M HERE NOW TO KEEP YOU SAFE!

misses. Luckily us ravens have been here to prevent any outright catastrophes!

The coronation ceremony is over 1,200 years old, and England is the only European country in which the monarch is still crowned in an ancient coronation rite. Every king or queen since William the Conqueror has been crowned in the same sumptuous ceremony at Westminster Abbey in London.

The Crown Jewels include St Edward's Crown and the Imperial State Crown, as well as some beautiful pieces of regalia such as the Sovereign's Sceptre with Cross and the Sovereign's Orb. The Jewels have been kept here at the Tower of London for hundreds of years. Occasionally some of them are taken away for a state occasion, like the State Opening of Parliament.

Sovereign is another word for king or queen. The sovereign's regalia are the sacred and precious objects, including the crown, that symbolize the monarchy and are used in the coronation ceremony.

ABBEY ANTICS

In the very old days – not even Groggie was around then – the Crown Jewels weren't kept at the Tower. Monarchs had their own crowns and ornaments that they wore whenever they pleased. When they weren't wearing them, they locked them away in reinforced rooms in their palaces. However, the most special crowns and ornaments, used only for coronations, were kept at Westminster Abbey in London and guarded by monks.

Eventually all the various crowns and ornaments were moved to Westminster for safe keeping. But during Edward I's reign (1272–1307) dastardly thieves broke in and stole some valuables, although luckily they missed the priceless coronation items.

Shocked officials decided that some of the royal treasures would be safer behind the five-metre-thick walls of the White Tower, here at the Tower of London. The precious objects were locked up in the basement with no less than forty-nine keys! (We kept a beady eye on them too.)

However, the Westminster monks insisted the sacred coronation items must remain in the holy confines of the Abbey. And there they stayed, until in 1649, they met a terrible fate.

46, 47...

MELTDOWN

Now Groggie told you at the beginning that the Crown Jewels are real. And he's right! But the ones you see in the Jewel House today aren't the same ones that were nearly stolen from Edward I. Apart from a few charming medieval pieces that have survived, the Crown Jewels today mostly date back to 1661.

This is because Charles I (1625–1649) sold off some of the Crown's treasures during his reign to pay his bills. In fact, the king was so careless with his spending and so reluctant to listen to Parliament that he made many enemies. His supporters ended up fighting his opponents in the Civil War. Charles I lost the war – and his head – in 1649. For the period of time between 1649 and 1660, known as the Interregnum, there was no king or queen.

The man who won the Civil War was Oliver Cromwell. He was called the Lord Protector but, if you ask me, he didn't do much protecting – especially not of the Crown Jewels. The Jewels are one of the monarchy's most powerful symbols and Cromwell believed that by destroying them, he would show everyone the monarchy was over for good. On his orders, the ancient crowns were smashed up, the jewels prised out and sold, and the remaining gold melted down in the Mint to make coins.

When Cromwell died, his son became Lord Protector, but was a weaker ruler. Soon the monarchy was restored and Charles II (1660–1685) took the throne. He ordered a new set of Crown Jewels for his coronation in 1661. This new set of regalia joined the other treasures at the Tower, where it has been ever since. Many of the objects are still used in coronations today.

> *The most valuable of the original jewels to be destroyed by Cromwell was the Tudor Crown. It weighed as much as a new-born baby, and was set with 28 diamonds, 19 sapphires, 37 rubies and 168 pearls.*

DIAMONDS AREN'T FOR EVER!

BIRDS OF A FEATHER

You will see a dove perched on top of the Sovereign's Sceptre with Dove, one of the Crown Jewels made for Charles II's coronation. If you ask me, I think it should really be a raven on there. We've done far more over the years to protect the sovereign than any dove EVER could.

There's also a dove on the sceptre made for Queen Mary II's (1689–1694) joint coronation with William III (1689–1702). The dove's outstretched wings show that Mary was a queen in her own right, not just a queen consort (the wife of a king). But this beautiful sceptre wasn't needed again after her coronation, and it was soon lost. It was found over a hundred years later in 1814, covered in dust at the back of a cupboard.

STOP THIEF!

And that's not the only time the Crown Jewels have been nearly lost or stolen. From 1669, they were kept on the ground floor of the Martin Tower. Visitors could come and see them, and even hold them if they paid a fee to Talbot Edwards, the Jewel Keeper. What were those feather-brained people thinking? Something was bound to go wrong…

In 1671, "Colonel" Thomas Blood, who was more of a crook than a colonel, arrived at the Tower, disguised as a priest. Over the course of several visits, Blood made friends with Edwards and lulled him into a false sense of security. Blood then returned with his son, also called Thomas, a friend, Robert Perot, and a well-known thug, Richard Halliwell.

They asked to see the Jewels, then bashed poor Edwards over

I KNEW THOSE SKINNY BREECHES WERE A BAD IDEA!

the head and tied him up. Perot grabbed the Sovereign's Orb and stuffed it down his trousers, while Blood squashed the Imperial State Crown so it would fit under his cloak. Young Thomas was about to saw the Sovereign's Sceptre in half so he could carry it out in a bag when Edwards' son appeared unexpectedly, back from the army after several years abroad. The alarm was raised and Blood's gang made a run for it.

Perot, slowed down by the Orb in his trousers, was caught immediately, the others were captured before they reached the Tower gates. Unbelievably, Charles II pardoned all three men for reasons that remain mysterious to this day. Darlings, I would have had their heads on the block!

The Sovereign's Orb, which is hollow, was dented in the robbery and had to be repaired.

FROWN JEWELS

Security was tightened after Colonel Blood's attempt, but this
meant jewel-viewing lost a little of its sparkle. A visitor to the
Tower in 1710 described how he had to sit on a hard bench in
a "gloomy and cramped den" to view the Crown Jewels, which
were kept behind thick iron bars.

As the years went by, things didn't get better. In 1821,
one traveller called seeing the Jewels a "farce", writing that
"a ghastly old woman takes some sceptres and crowns out of
a couple of old boxes, shows them through an iron grate
and chants with a shrill voice the list and story of these
wonderful curiosities."

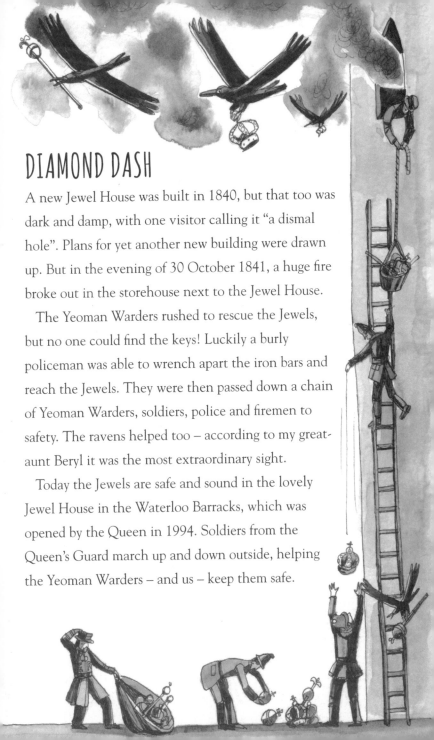

DIAMOND DASH

A new Jewel House was built in 1840, but that too was dark and damp, with one visitor calling it "a dismal hole". Plans for yet another new building were drawn up. But in the evening of 30 October 1841, a huge fire broke out in the storehouse next to the Jewel House.

The Yeoman Warders rushed to rescue the Jewels, but no one could find the keys! Luckily a burly policeman was able to wrench apart the iron bars and reach the Jewels. They were then passed down a chain of Yeoman Warders, soldiers, police and firemen to safety. The ravens helped too – according to my great-aunt Beryl it was the most extraordinary sight.

Today the Jewels are safe and sound in the lovely Jewel House in the Waterloo Barracks, which was opened by the Queen in 1994. Soldiers from the Queen's Guard march up and down outside, helping the Yeoman Warders – and us – keep them safe.

CORONATION CATASTROPHES

I get a bit twitchy whenever the Crown Jewels have to leave the Tower for a state occasion. Look what happened at James II's (1685–1688) coronation. One of the jewels on the top of the Sovereign's Sceptre with Cross fell off during the ceremony. Luckily the Earl of Peterborough noticed and picked it up off the floor. The sceptre was damaged again during George IV's (1820–1830) wild coronation banquet in 1821, and had to be repaired after the event.

Then poor about-to-be Queen Victoria (1837–1901) suffered an unfortunate incident at her coronation in 1838. When the Archbishop of Canterbury tried to put on her specially made Coronation Ring, he discovered it was much too small. There was nothing anyone could do. The eighteen-year-old Victoria had to keep looking serene as the archbishop rammed it on to her finger.

IS THAT ONE'S CROWN OR A VICTORIA SPONGE?

It was red faces all round at the State Opening of Parliament in 1845, also presided over by Queen Victoria. The elderly Duke of Argyll, who had been carrying the Imperial State Crown on a cushion, let it fall to the ground "with a great crash". The queen later described her crown as "all crushed, & squashed, looking like a pudding that had sat down".

Today when the Imperial State Crown is taken from the Tower for the State Opening of Parliament, a little note saying "In Use" is put in the glass case in the Jewel House while the crown is absent. Of course, these days the regalia is transported to and from the Tower with the utmost care and the highest security, and so far, thanks to my beady eye, nothing has gone wrong.

Victoria became queen in 1837 when she was eighteen years old.

BUTTERFINGERS!

CORONATION CHAMPIONS

Despite some silly sovereigns, attempted robberies and terrible blunders, the Crown Jewels have survived to this day. St Edward's Crown, the Imperial State Crown, the Sovereign's Sceptre with Cross and the Sovereign's Orb are among the

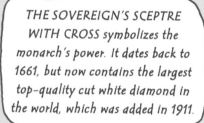

THE SOVEREIGN'S SCEPTRE WITH CROSS symbolizes the monarch's power. It dates back to 1661, but now contains the largest top-quality cut white diamond in the world, which was added in 1911.

THE IMPERIAL STATE CROWN was made in 1937 and is worn at the end of the coronation ceremony and for the State Opening of Parliament every year.

most symbolic of all the Crown Jewels, because they are the objects used in the coronation ceremony. But there are many other marvellous pieces that you must come and see for yourself in the Jewel House.

LOOK OUT FOR ME WHEN YOU VISIT. I NEVER MIND POSING FOR A PHOTO!

ST EDWARD'S CROWN is only ever used during a coronation for the actual moment of crowning the new monarch. It was made for Charles II's coronation to replace a crown thought to belong to Edward the Confessor.

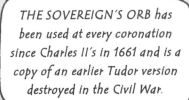

THE SOVEREIGN'S ORB has been used at every coronation since Charles II's in 1661 and is a copy of an earlier Tudor version destroyed in the Civil War.

CROWN JEWELS CALAMITIES QUIZ

1. Why did Oliver Cromwell melt down the Crown Jewels?
a) He was short of money.
b) He disliked shiny things.
c) He wanted to destroy the symbols of monarchy.
d) He wanted to make a new set of Crown Jewels for himself.

2. What is the name of the unit used to measure the purity of gold?
a) Carrot
b) Carat
c) Coronet
d) Clarinet

3. Why did George V tie a piece of red cotton to the front of St Edward's Crown before his coronation?
a) So he could hang it up neatly afterwards.
b) To ensure he put it on the right way round.
c) For good luck.
d) So he chose the right crown.

4. Why couldn't Robert Perot, Thomas Blood's accomplice, run away after their attempt to steal the Crown Jewels?
a) He had a wooden leg.
b) The Jewel House Keeper's dog bit him.
c) He had the Sovereign's Orb stuffed down his trousers.
d) He fell into the moat.

5. Which two of these are NOT parts of a crown?
a) Tiara
b) Arch
c) Cap
d) Woggle

CHAPTER THREE
A RUFF LIFE

Find out why the Yeoman Warders are called "Beefeaters" and discover what they do at the Tower.

I say, I say, I say, Grog – how does a Yeoman Warder run in full dress uniform?

I don't know, Gripp. How does a Yeoman Warder run in full dress uniform?

I don't know. I've never actually seen it happen! HA, HA, HA!

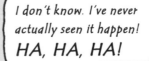

Oh, you are naughty! Now stop joking around, Mr G, and tell us about the Yeoman Warders. I've seen you eyeing up those shiny buttons and don't try and pretend you wouldn't love to try on the Constable's hat.

You've got me there, Grog. I do love a nice uniform and the ones worn here are fabulous. The guardians of the Tower, the Yeoman Warders, have a wonderful red and gold uniform for special occasions. It's all polished boots and shiny buttons, and all sorts of wonderful hats. In fact, the only thing that's a bit slapdash is the terrible clothes you tourists wear!

GREAT GUARDIANS

The Yeoman Warders are the jolly characters you see patrolling around in those lovely uniforms and funny hats. There are thirty-seven Yeoman Warders, both men and women, and they are the Tower's ceremonial guardians. That means they keep you tourists in order on a daily basis. They also have to make sure everything runs like clockwork if there is an important occasion, like a royal visit. They also know lots about history – though not quite as much as we do – so they give guided tours. But if you want a really juicy historical titbit – ask us!

A DAY IN THE LIFE OF A YEOMAN WARDER

There is a Chief Yeoman Warder. His second in command is called the Yeoman Gaoler. Some of the warders have special duties or titles – like the Ravenmaster, whose job it is to look after us. All the Yeoman Warders live here at the Tower.

To become a Yeoman Warder you have to be over forty years old and have served in the Armed Forces with an honourable record for at least twenty-two years. You also have to be awarded medals for long service and good conduct. That means that the Yeoman Warders aren't quite spring chicks when they come to us, and between you and me, I think they are glad we're here to help keep you all entertained!

WHAT'S THE BEEF?

The Yeoman Warders have been at the Tower for centuries. They were originally part of the Yeomen of the Guard – the king's (there were no queens in those days) personal bodyguard, who travelled everywhere with him keeping him safe. The Yeomen of the Guard originally wore a simple uniform, known as a livery. Under Henry VII (1485–1509), it was green in colour. But his son, Henry VIII (1509–1547), decided he wanted a more regal look for his bodyguard. He changed the Yeomen of the Guard's livery to a striking red, gold and white.

Henry VIII rarely stayed at the Tower after 1533, preferring his more comfortable palaces at Whitehall and Hampton Court. But he didn't want the Tower to be unprotected, so he decided that some of the men in the Yeomen of the Guard would stay at the Tower to watch it. These were the very first Yeoman Warders. You might also hear them called "Beefeaters". The story goes that this is because, as members of the king's bodyguard, they were allowed to eat as much beef as they wanted.

In the early days, the Yeoman Warders at the Tower weren't allowed to wear the smart red, gold and white uniform of the Yeomen of the Guard. And unsurprisingly they were quite frustrated. But in the 1500s, an influential prisoner at the Tower, the Earl of Suffolk, offered to grant the Yeoman Warders a favour if they treated him well. So they requested to wear the same red and gold uniform as the rest of the Yeomen of the Guard – and they still wear it today.

The uniforms of the Yeomen of the Guard and that of the Yeoman Warders of the Tower have a few small differences. The Yeomen of the Guard have a sash across the front of their jackets, called a baldrick, used to hold a musket. Yeoman Warders have an epaulette, an ornamental decoration, on their left shoulder.

DRESSING UP

YO, MAN!

Now I've noticed some of you having a little chuckle at the Yeoman Warders' uniforms. But I don't understand why! I'd love to wear that uniform every day – and I much prefer it to the scruffy clothes you wear! Don't poke me with your selfie sticks, but I do sometimes think you could dress for the occasion and make a bit more effort to look spick and span when you visit us.

The Yeoman Warders certainly look the part. Today they have two uniforms which they wear on different occasions: a red and gold state "dress" uniform and a blue "undress" uniform. In the past, the Yeoman Warders used to wear the red dress uniform every day. But during the nineteenth century, as more and more jobs were done by machine, the soot from the factories made London filthy. The dirty air damaged the fabric of the Yeoman Warders' expensive uniforms.

In 1858, mindful that it was getting expensive to keep buying new uniforms, Queen Victoria (1837–1901) asked Sir Robert Peel, founder of the Metropolitan Police, to design a new everyday uniform in sensible dark blue, which wouldn't show the dirt. This is the undress uniform that you see the

Yeoman Warders wearing when you visit the Tower.

These days, the state dress uniform is only worn when the Yeoman Warders are on duty at special occasions at the Tower – events that the Resident Governor and Royal Family attend – or royal weddings and funerals which happen elsewhere.

In Victorian London, the fumes from factories created fogs that were so thick people would walk into the Thames because they couldn't see where they were going.

There is also a "semi-state" dress uniform, which is the full red dress jacket and Tudor bonnet, but worn with ordinary trousers and boots. It's worn on important occasions at the Tower which the Royal Family don't attend, like the Gun Salutes, which are fired to celebrate a royal birth or anniversary.

DRESSED TO IMPRESS

Yeoman Warders only wear their full dress uniforms seven or eight times a year.

Ruff made from starched linen (which makes it itchy).

Embroidery of the rose of England, the thistle of Scotland and the shamrock of Ireland.

Garter

Rosette

Britches

STATE DRESS UNIFORM

UNDRESS UNIFORM

HATS OFF

People at the Tower also get to wear some very handsome hats. Here's a guide to who wears what.

TUDOR BONNETS are worn by the Yeoman Warders as part of their dress uniform. They are made from black velvet and decorated with red, white and blue ribbons.

BLUE UNDRESS HATS are worn by the Yeoman Warders for everyday duties. They are made of barathea – the same material used to make school blazers.

A BLACK BICORN HAT is worn by the Constable of the Tower, the highest ranking official at the Tower of London, and is decorated with white and red swan feathers.

BEARSKINS are worn by the regiments of guardsmen who protect the Crown Jewels. They are made from the pelt of bears.

TIGHT TIMINGS

I have a good chum among the Yeoman Warders – I won't tell you his name in case he gets into trouble – who says that it can take up to two hours for a new recruit to put on the full state dress uniform. Supposedly it gets quicker once you know what you're doing. We can always tell something exciting is happening when we see the Yeoman Warders appear on duty, pulling at their ruffs, shouting for safety pins, as they've forgotten to sew on missing buttons, and fumbling with their medals, trying to look ready for action.

It's also quite difficult for the Yeoman Warders to move at any great speed once they're finally buttoned into their uniform. You will never see a Yeoman Warder actually *run* in full dress uniform. That would be far too undignified! So they proceed at what is known as a "measured" pace towards any trouble, which hopefully will be over by the time they eventually arrive. I tell you, I can flap faster, even with my wings clipped!

KEEP CALM AND CARRION!

The Ceremony of the
Keys has taken place nearly
every night since 1555.

IN THE RED

Looking fabulous comes at a
price. The Yeoman Warders'
uniforms aren't cheap. The
state dress uniform costs around
£4,000 and there are
thirty-seven Yeoman Warders.

Each uniform is adjusted so it is a perfect fit.

For the ancient Ceremony of the Keys, a ritual which involves
locking the Tower's gates with the sovereign's keys every night,
the Chief Yeoman Warder has to wear a special coat called a
Watch Coat. These cost around £400 each.

LOOKING BLUE

The blue undress uniform is cheaper. The uniforms have to be
replaced every eighteen months or so, as the fabric fades in the
sun and is rotted away by sweat. Still, each uniform costs around
£1,600. It comes in a lighter summer weight, so the Yeoman
Warders can stay cool, and also a heavier winter weight for when
it gets nippy. But from the mutterings I've heard, the uniforms
aren't always the most comfortable things to wear.

HOT STUFF

There's no doubt that the Yeoman Warders look a picture. But what's it actually like to wear one of their uniforms? I asked my chum and he told me that they are itchy, scratchy and boiling hot – and that's at the best of times! So imagine what it's like on summer days. When we're in our birdbaths and you're wandering about happily in your flip-flops, the Yeoman Warders are stiffly standing to attention in the blazing sun wearing a belted overcoat, trousers and a hat. But you'll never hear them complain (except perhaps when there are only ravens in earshot). After all, it's a great honour to serve at the Tower.

OOH, I'D LOVE AN ICE CREAM!

MORE BEEF

The only other tiny problem is that the Yeoman Warders do rather change shape while they serve at the Tower (oh, yes you do!). They tend to grow – not upwards, but *outwards*, so it's essential their uniforms can be altered. They might not eat so much beef these days, but I've seen them munch through the biscuits on a tea break. Compared to their previously active lives in the Armed Forces, they slow down once they come to the Tower. "Cuddly" is perhaps a good description – but *shh!* – don't tell them I said that!

A RUFF LIFE QUIZ

1. What must a Yeoman Warder have to qualify for the job?
a) An obsession with dressing up
b) A very loud voice
c) At least twenty-two years' honourable military service
d) A wicked sense of humour

2. An image of a Yeoman Warder appears on a brand of what?
a) Tomato ketchup
b) Mouthwash
c) Gin
d) Crisps

3. What essential equipment does a Yeoman Warder always carry?
a) Handcuffs
b) Emergency biscuit ration
c) A stun gun
d) Safety pins

4. The Yeoman Warders' blue "undress" uniforms were introduced in Victorian times because:
a) they didn't show the dirt.
b) the expensive red uniforms were being ruined by pollution.
c) the blue matched Queen Victoria's eyes.
d) they supported Chelsea.

5. Yeoman Warders carry out the Ceremony of the Keys at the Tower every night. Which of these is NOT a ceremony held at the Tower?
a) Beating the Bounds
b) The Constable's Dues
c) Gun Salutes
d) The Ravens' Annual Dental Check-Up

CHAPTER FOUR
ATTACK AND DEFENCE

Find out how the Tower was attacked and very nearly conquered.

ATTENTION!
Edgar "Colonel" Sopper has some stories to share about attacks on the Tower. He's a bit of a history buff who loves reading about old wars. And he knows only too well that despite its massive defences, the Tower hasn't always been invincible...

At ease, Officer Grog!
Colonel Sopper here! I'll have you know that the Tower is run like a well-oiled machine today. Wasn't always so, however! Few centuries ago, it was a bit of a shambles, I can tell you. Let me tell you about the most disgraceful military lapses and defence disasters.

FORMIDABLE FORTRESS

When William the Conqueror (1066–1087) gave orders for the Tower to be built in the 1070s, there had never been such a strong and impressive fortress in all of England. It was the tallest building in London and it was meant to strike fear into the hearts of possible attackers. Later kings made the Tower even bigger, adding new outer walls, towers and even a moat. But their new defences didn't always do the job.

OH BROTHER

Let's start with Richard I (1189–1199), who was also known as the "Lionheart". He was a terrific chap and top-notch soldier. A king who truly knew how to lead his troops! But when he wasn't off fighting, he spent most of his time in France, rather than here in chilly Blighty. While he was away, he left the Tower in the care of the Constable of the Tower, a French chap called William Longchamp. The English nobles didn't like him much, as he was a bit of a big-headed so-and-so, and supposedly only spoke French and Latin.

Longchamp doubled the size of the Tower and built a moat of "great depth" around it to strengthen its defences. He thought a moat would protect the Tower, as it would mean no one could reach its walls without having to swim across it. But when Longchamp let in the river water from the Thames, the buffoon realized the moat wasn't actually deep enough. Invaders could simply wade across!

Richard I's sneaky younger brother, Prince John, then saw a chance to get rid of the unpopular Longchamp and take the throne himself. In 1191, he attacked the Tower. Longchamp and his men retreated behind the Tower's new defences. But Longchamp had made a big mistake. He hadn't stocked up on provisions for his men inside the walls. So Prince John's forces were able to lay siege to the Tower, and after holding out for a few days, Longchamp's men were forced to surrender or starve to death.

Find out what happened to Longchamp in Chapter Six.

Longchamp fled the country and Prince John took charge of the Tower until Richard I returned to England in 1194. John was able to persuade his brother to forgive him and was named his successor. He became king in 1199.

MOAT MISERY

King John's son, Henry III (1216–1272), made the Tower even bigger and stronger during his reign. He built nine new towers on the north, east and west sides and a massive fortified wall, called a curtain wall, to link them all together.

Henry III also decided to dig a new moat and hired the Flemish engineer John le Fossur (Flemish for "the ditch digger") to do the job. He did *actually* manage to make the moat fill with water from the Thames. However, the water didn't drain back out again. Not a problem you might think – except that as the Tower got bigger, more toilets were built, and most of these emptied into the moat. Add to this, rotting food and dead animals and you might say that the resulting stink was actually the Tower's best defence!

WET PAINT

In 1240, Henry III had the huge central tower painted white, which is how the White Tower – one of the world's most famous castle keeps – got its name.

WHAT A STINKER

WOBBLY WALLS

Unfortunately Henry III's new walls weren't as strong as he had hoped. A huge new gateway near the Beauchamp Tower collapsed in April 1240. A chap at the time wrote that "… the stonework of a certain noble gateway which the king had constructed in the most opulent fashion collapsed, as if struck by an earthquake…"

The furious king immediately had the wall rebuilt. But a priest claimed a saint had come to him in a dream and told him the wall would fall down again in exactly a year's time. And would you believe it, according to the old records, "the walls … collapsed irreparably" a year to the day.

Poppycock, you might think! And for hundreds of years everyone thought that this was just a story. But then an archaeological excavation of the moat revealed a massive stone platform, which sloped at a wild angle, very near to the existing stone wall. The archaeologists were able to confirm that the stonework dated back to the thirteenth century, so this story seems to be more fact than fiction.

PESKY PEASANTS

With all this work building walls, you would have thought the Tower would have been almost impenetrable. But no! There was a shambolic incident during the Peasants' Revolt in 1381 that I must tell you about.

When Richard II (1377–1399) came to the throne he was only ten years old. It was a difficult time to be a king because expensive foreign wars had nearly bankrupted the country and the Black Death had killed hundreds of thousands of people. The poorest people – the peasants – had no food or money and they were growing increasingly angry with the king. So in 1381 the peasants started a rebellion against Richard II and his government.

The Black Death was a terrible disease, or "plague", spread by rat fleas. It killed between 75 million and 200 million people across the world during 1330–1350.

WHY DON'T YOU FLEA, RAT!

One of their leaders, Wat Tyler, marched on London with a raggedy but determined band of 20,000 men. Wat Tyler and his men burnt down government ministers' houses and plundered London. Richard II, now aged fourteen, and his mother, Princess Joan, who was known as the Fair Maid of Kent because of her beauty, fled to the Tower, where they should have been safe. Instead it was a fiasco!

Soon hundreds of rowdy rebel peasants had gathered outside the Tower. Brave Richard II rode out to try to talk to Wat Tyler and bring the rebellion to an end. But some stupid idiot left the Tower's gates open behind the king. Four hundred poorly armed peasants took their chance and ran inside.

The guards were completely taken by surprise and didn't put up a fight. Some people said they might even have sympathized with the peasants. Shameful behaviour! One gang burst into the royal apartments, surprising the king's mother and her ladies-in-waiting. The rebels even had the cheek to demand kisses from the Fair Maid. Terrified, Princess Joan fainted and was carried to safety by her servants.

Another group pursued their real target – the Archbishop of Canterbury and the king's Chancellor, Simon Sudbury. The rebels found him at prayer in St John's Chapel in the White Tower and showed no mercy. Sudbury was dragged out of the Tower and beheaded over a log of wood on Tower Hill. It took the axeman eight blows to sever his head, which was then impaled on a spike and mounted on London Bridge.

Meanwhile, the young king tried to calm the situation. But in the confusion, the rebel leader Wat Tyler was killed. Richard II then rode forward and shouted, "You shall have no captain but me!" He apparently agreed to the rebels' demands and they believed him. With their leader dead, the rebels gave up and meekly returned home.

But Richard went back on his word, and a few months later, his soldiers rounded up and hanged lots of the rebels.

LAST-DITCH ATTEMPT

After that disaster, the Tower's defences held fast for hundreds of years. But the moat was still causing problems. When Queen Victoria (1837–1901) was on the throne in 1841, the moat was "impregnated with putrid animal and excrementitious matter … and emitting a most obnoxious smell".

Not only was it smelly, it was dangerous too. Several soldiers who had been posted at the Tower died and about eighty had to be sent to hospital, possibly because they had drunk the filthy water. Outbreaks in the local area of a dangerous disease called cholera were also blamed on the moat. The Duke of Wellington, the Constable of the Tower at that time, finally decided that enough was enough. In 1843, the moat was drained to create the dry ditch that you can see today.

ATTACK AND DEFENCE QUIZ

1. **William Longchamp had to surrender the Tower in 1191 after a siege because:**
   a) he got scared.
   b) he forgot to stock up on food.
   c) he needed the loo.
   d) he got bored in the Tower.

2. **Which of these is NOT a weapon of attack or defence?**
   a) A trebuchet
   b) A mace
   c) A muskrat
   d) A crossbow

3. **Which of these was NOT a problem with the Tower's moat?**
   a) It wasn't deep enough.
   b) It didn't drain properly.
   c) It had a crocodile living in it.
   d) It was filled with dirty water.

4. **Which one of these was NOT thought to cure the Black Death?**
   a) Rubbing onions on the boils
   b) Being pecked by a peacock
   c) Eating treacle
   d) Rubbing a chopped-up snake over the infected body

5. **During the Peasants' Revolt of 1381, Richard II's mother, the Fair Maid of Kent, fainted because:**
   a) her corset had been laced too tightly.
   b) the stink of the moat was too much for her.
   c) a peasant wanted to kiss her.
   d) she was scared that her son was in danger.

CHAPTER FIVE
GREAT ESCAPES

Learn who escaped from the Tower and how they managed to sneak past the Yeoman Warders.

> Now we all know the Tower of London is a terrifying place of torture, torment and imprisonment. But what was it ACTUALLY like to be a prisoner here? Would you believe it, the Tower's very first prisoner escaped.

> Who could blame him? It's not much fun ALWAYS being stuck behind these massive walls!

> Well, you know all about breaking out of the Tower, Munin! Don't think I've forgotten that time you escaped to Greenwich Park. But you didn't last long, did you? You let the Ravenmaster come and catch you. We all know you secretly missed us!

> **I wasn't missing you!** I was missing the blood-soaked biscuits! Now let me tell you about some more great escapes.

LOCK-UP

Only the most important or dangerous prisoners were kept captive at the Tower. These prisoners were the enemy of the king or queen and were often being held on charges of treason and were in danger of being executed. So it's no surprise that they wanted to escape! Now from the outside, the Tower looks like it would be impossible to escape from. It's got a deep moat, huge walls and giant gates. But it's not actually as secure as Grog and Colonel Sopper would have you believe. As several prisoners showed, all you needed was a little bit of ingenuity and a whole lot of luck – just like when I went on my Greenwich Park adventure!

The ravens at the Tower today have their flight feathers regularly trimmed to stop them flying away.

I'M GONNA HAVE A MEAN TIME IN GREENWICH!

PRISON PARTY

The first person held as a prisoner at the Tower was Ranulf Flambard in the twelfth century. He was the Bishop of Durham and he was imprisoned in 1100 by Henry I (1100–1135) for stealing. But because he was wealthy and influential, he wasn't thrown in a dark dungeon. Instead he was given a cell at the top of the White Tower and plenty of delicious food and wine.

Flambard made friends with his guards by sharing his food and drink with them. So no one was suspicious when Flambard was sent a big barrel of wine to celebrate the feast of Candlemas in February 1101. Flambard got his guards drunk. Once they were snoring, he pulled out a rope that had been hidden in the bottom of the barrel. He tied the rope to a window bar of his cell and climbed out. His friends were waiting outside the Tower with horses to make a speedy getaway. Flambard escaped to Normandy, but he was soon back in favour with the king, so he returned to England and lived out his life happily as a free man.

ZZZZZ

KNOCK-OUT

Alcohol also played a part in the escape of another prisoner about two hundred years later. The rebel nobleman Roger Mortimer was sentenced to life imprisonment in 1322 for trying to overthrow Edward II (1307–1327). But he was allowed to have food and wine sent to his cell. One evening, Mortimer invited no less than the Constable of the Tower and his guards to have a drink with him.

Naughty Mortimer laced their wine with a strong sleeping potion – so strong, in fact, that the Constable of the Tower was still ill five days later! Once the guards were unconscious, the deputy Constable of the Tower, who was secretly a friend of Mortimer's, led him out of his cell and down through the kitchens. The two men escaped over the outer wall of the Tower with a rope ladder and climbed down to the river, where their friends were waiting in a boat. They fled abroad, much to the utter fury of the king.

PAMPERED PRISONERS

Being a prisoner at the Tower wasn't *always* bad. For certain high-ranking prisoners, the Tower was actually a very comfortable and cosy place. King John Balliol of Scotland was imprisoned by Edward I (1272–1307) at the end of the thirteenth century and spent three very pleasant years at the Tower. He certainly wasn't lonely, as with him came:

2 squires
1 huntsman
1 barber
1 chaplain
1 chapel clerk
and several assistants
2 grooms
2 chamberlains
1 tailor
1 laundress
3 pages
2 greyhounds
10 hunting dogs

IT'S A BIT OF A SQUEEZE.

Kings were well treated in prison because they were rich and influential – and might get back into power one day.

LUXURY CONFINEMENT

Another high-ranking prisoner, King John II of France, was
so well treated at the Tower that he came back for more! The
French king was captured at the Battle of Poitiers in 1356 and
brought to England, but there was no dank dungeon for him.
Instead, he was given a lavishly decorated chamber. His many
servants and youngest son were also given lodgings near to the
Tower – at great expense. And he wasn't even confined to his
cell. The lucky prisoner was allowed into the city to go shopping. If only the Ravenmaster would let me do that!

When he was released, he threw a huge banquet in honour
of his "hosts", Edward III (1327–1377) and his queen Philippa,
to say thank you. But the French never actually paid the
enormous ransom that was due to Edward III on the prisoner's
release. So John chivalrously agreed to return to captivity in
England and remained in the Tower for the rest of his life. He
must have missed the shopping!

SPARE MY FLUSHES

Toilets at the Tower were a square-topped shaft with hole, located on the outside walls. The shaft went straight into the moat.

But being imprisoned at the Tower wasn't always luxurious. There was one poor prisoner who must have *really* wished he could have flown over the walls. Henry Howard, Earl of Surrey, made enemies of the powerful Seymour family. They convinced Henry VIII (1509–1547) that Howard was plotting to seize the throne after his death. Thrown into a Tower cell in 1547 and left to rot, Howard noticed that the shaft of his latrine (an old-fashioned toilet) ran from his room into the moat below. It was just about wide (and slippery) enough for a man to squeeze through.

Howard had very nearly escaped, but a guard noticed his empty bed and discovered him wriggling down the shaft. His belly was too large for him to be able to squeeze through and he had got stuck! Howard was executed on Tower Hill in January 1547, just nine days before Henry VIII died.

HE'LL NEED TO WASH HIS HAIR TONIGHT!

INVISIBLE INK

Father John Gerard was a priest thought to be a danger to the ageing Elizabeth I (1558–1603), so he was imprisoned in 1594. The queen wanted to find out who his accomplices were, so he was tortured by being hung from the wrists in chains, but he refused to give his captors any information. Instead he persuaded a guard to bring him oranges, which, although expensive, were unlikely to arouse any suspicion. But Gerard knew that when dry, orange juice was invisible on paper, only reappearing when heated over a flame. He wrote secret messages to his supporters on the outside, using orange juice as ink.

He also used this ingenious method to write letters to another priest, John Arden, who was imprisoned in the Cradle Tower. The two men were allowed to celebrate Mass together, and used this time to hatch a plot. On 5 October 1597, Gerard and Arden descended from the Cradle Tower, swung across the moat on a rope and jumped down into a boat waiting on the Thames below. Gerard escaped capture and lived the rest of his days a wanted man.

TOWER TORTURE

There are many terrible tales about torture here and behind the legends are some true stories. Torture was used in the sixteenth and seventeenth centuries as a way to get information from prisoners, rather than as a punishment. Sometimes just the

threat of it was enough to break a cold, hungry and frightened prisoner – so it's no surprise people tried to escape!

There were several different ways prisoners were tortured. Some people were hung from the walls or ceiling by the wrists from manacles. Or their arms and legs were stretched on a device called a rack. There was also an instrument known as the Scavenger's Daughter, which squashed the prisoner's legs against their chest. This was meant to be so painful that prisoners could only bear an hour before confessing.

TERRIFYING TOURISTS

By a strange coincidence, the first prisoner of the Tower, Ranulf Flambard, arrived on 15 August 1100. Over 800 years later, on 15 August 1941, the German spy Josef Jakobs was executed by firing squad, the last prisoner to die here. Today there are no prisoners kept at the Tower and the only torture is listening to Grog and the Ravenmaster tell their boring stories to the tourists. Maybe I'll be making another break for it soon!

GREAT ESCAPES QUIZ

1. Which two of these Johns were locked up in the Tower?
a) King John II of France
b) Father John Gerard
c) John Travolta
d) King John I of England

2. Which of these was NOT requested by King John Balliol of Scotland during his imprisonment at the Tower?
a) A huntsman
b) A laundress
c) A barber
d) An iPad

3. Which fruit juice did Father John Gerard use as "invisible" ink?
a) Orange
b) Banana
c) Ugli fruit
d) Lemon

4. Which one of these is an instrument of torture?
a) Effingham's Mother
b) Framlingham's Father
c) Scavenger's Daughter
d) Aldringham's Uncle

5. Who is supposed to have murdered the Tower's most famous prisoners – the Princes in the Tower?
a) Cardinal Wolsey
b) Richard III
c) Elizabeth I
d) Mary I

CHAPTER SIX
COSTUME DRAMAS

Discover how dressing up at the Tower
was a matter of life or death.

Now you already know how much Gripp
likes dressing up. He also loves to play a
part. In fact, he knows everything there is
to know about dressing up at the Tower!

WANT TO HEAR A JOKE,
GROG? Two Elizabethan courtiers
are having a fight on the Wharf. Looks
like things are getting ruff!

Thank goodness your acting is
better than your jokes, Mr G!

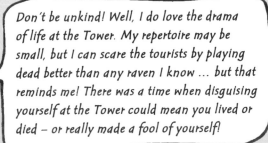

Don't be unkind! Well, I do love the drama
of life at the Tower. My repertoire may be
small, but I can scare the tourists by playing
dead better than any raven I know ... but that
reminds me! There was a time when disguising
yourself at the Tower could mean you lived or
died – or really made a fool of yourself!

PLAY-ACTING

Now there's no doubt there have been some very dramatic escapes in the Tower's history. But sometimes it just wasn't possible for prisoners to do the daring deeds Munin told you all about in Chapter Five. After all, it's not that easy to climb down ropes or write messages in invisible ink! But some prisoners knew how to play a different game and trick the Yeoman Warders. By disguising themselves, they could sneak out of the Tower unnoticed. After all, there's nothing like a little bit of dressing up to create a whole lot of distraction!

DRESSING DOWN

In 1191, a very unpopular Constable of the Tower named William Longchamp was forced to surrender the Tower. Prince John, Richard I's (1189–1199) naughty younger brother, had attacked and besieged the Tower and Longchamp was defeated. Fearing for his life, he fled to Dover, hoping to escape to France, his home country.

At Dover, Longchamp attempted to sneak on board a boat to France. But he didn't speak English, only French or Latin. His expensive clothes and terrible English accent soon made people rather suspicious of the stranger.

Colonel Sopper tells you more about Longchamp and the siege in Chapter Four.

In desperation, Longchamp tried to board another boat by wearing different clothes. But each time he tried, his disguise failed to convince anyone – even when he wore a monk's long brown habit. Finally he tried dressing himself as a woman and suddenly found himself a lot more popular with the sailors!

Longchamp got so into character that he tried a bit of flirting and soon a fisherman began to flirt back! Eventually Longchamp managed to escape both England and his fishy suitor and arrived in France. He was exiled for a number of years, before being allowed by the king to return to England.

A HAIR-RAISING ATTEMPT

It wasn't just men who were a dab hand at disguises. Lady Arabella Stuart (who was fourth in line for the throne) and William Seymour got into BIG trouble for marrying without the royal permission of James I (1603–1625). William was sent straight to the Tower, while Arabella, being more royal and also a lady, was put under house arrest nearby. Together, they hatched a cunning escape plan. Arabella pretended to be ill and took to her bed. This made her guards less watchful and they left her alone. She then dressed up in men's clothes, sneaked out of the house, jumped on a horse (easier in breeches) and galloped into the night.

Meanwhile her husband William Seymour was still a prisoner in the Tower. He was sent a false beard, which he

I'M SKIRTING AROUND THE PROBLEM!

pretended he had grown himself!
Seymour demanded that his barber,
who was also a good friend, was
sent to the Tower to shave
him. When his barber arrived,
Seymour swiftly removed
the fake beard and swapped
clothes with the barber.

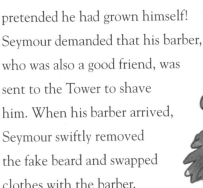

WEIRDY
BEARDY!

Together, they walked out of the Tower unchallenged.

But after all this careful plotting, Arabella and
William missed each other at their
agreed meeting place. They fled
abroad separately, but unluckily for
Arabella her boat was captured.
She was imprisoned in the
Tower, and eventually starved
herself to death in
1615. She never
saw her husband
again.

Some historians think
that Lady Arabella's
escapade might have
inspired famous
playwright William
Shakespeare's cross-
dressing heroine Imogen
in the play Cymbeline.

DARLING, YOU LOOK SO FABULOUS IN RED!

THE MAID IN A DRESS

One of the very final escape attempts from the Tower was possibly the most outrageous. In 1716, William Maxwell, Earl of Nithsdale, was imprisoned by George I (1714–1727) for his part in supporting the exiled king James II (1685–1688). On the eve of his execution, Lord Nithsdale's wife, Winifred, was allowed to visit him at the Tower, and the stage was set.

Winifred arrived at her husband's cell with her ladies-in-waiting. She was wearing an extra layer of clothing, including

Georgian ladies loved
using cosmetics, and
liked to have white faces
with dark eyebrows.

a large cloak
which still survives
today. She quickly dressed
her husband up as a woman,
even colouring his cheeks with
rouge and adding lipstick. With his head
bowed, Lord Nithsdale walked out of his cell with
the other ladies-in-waiting, who kept wailing and
crying to distract the guards. Nithsdale made it out of
the Tower to a waiting coach, which carried him to safety.
Brave Winifred remained in the cell and pretended to have
a conversation with her husband, mimicking his deep voice in
reply to her high-pitched lamenting. Finally she let herself out,
slammed the door and pleaded with the guards not to disturb
her husband, as he was deep in prayer.

Her elaborate plan worked. The couple were reunited and
escaped to Rome, where they lived the rest of their lives poor
but happy. According to some accounts, they even dressed up
occasionally for plays that they put on themselves.

WE'LL BE HERE ALL KNIGHT!

WHO TURNED OUT THE LIGHTS?

SUITS YOU!

And it's not just prisoners who liked dressing up. My great-grandfather Thor used to tell a fabulous story about one of the curators of the Royal Armouries at the Tower. The Royal Armouries has a collection of hundreds of pieces of armour, including those once worn by Henry VIII (1509–1547). Viscount Dillon, the curator, had a splendid pair of whiskers, and knew so much about military antiques that he even wrote a book about them. In fact, he loved armour so much that when the visitors left the Tower at the end of the day, he would dress up in the different suits and clank about in the White Tower dressed as a medieval knight. All in the interests of research, of course!

DRESS-UP DAYS

If you visit the Tower today, you'll often see actors dressed up in historical costumes, pretending to be knights and peasants. The visitors love this kind of show, so I always like to hop over to lend a bit of atmosphere to the proceedings – and possibly snack on an abandoned sandwich.

MMMMM...
EGG AND CRESS!

COSTUME DRAMAS QUIZ

1. **In which two disguises did William Longchamp NOT try to escape?**
   a) A monk
   b) A woman
   c) A mermaid
   d) A shell suit

2. **What was a farthingale?**
   a) A piece of harness
   b) An Elizabethan hairpiece
   c) A wired undergarment
   d) A medieval bicycle

3. **Who escaped from the Tower dressed as a woman?**
   a) William, Earl of Nithsdale
   b) Lady Winifred Nithsdale
   c) William Longchamp
   d) Lady Arabella Stuart

4. **What was in the powder that Georgian women used to whiten their faces?**
   a) Icing sugar
   b) Flour
   c) Lead
   d) Chalk

5. **Why did Viscount Dillon dress up in armour after hours?**
   a) He was trying to impress his girlfriend.
   b) He ran out of clean clothes.
   c) He wanted to scare the visitors.
   d) He loved armour.

CHAPTER SEVEN
MENAGERIE MADNESS

Find out about the animals that have lived at the Tower.

Although there is NO doubt we are the most important animals at the Tower, we can't claim to be the only ones to have lived here. The Tower has been home to all sorts of strange – and often very dangerous – creatures.

Just ask my great-uncle Bert! When that big leopard pounced, he was lucky to escape alive! But he was a brave bird, was my great-uncle!

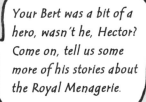

Your Bert was a bit of a hero, wasn't he, Hector? Come on, tell us some more of his stories about the Royal Menagerie.

All right then, Grog, I will! Now, I know the Ravenmaster tells the tourists not to feed us because we can be a bit over-enthusiastic with our beaks. But, believe you me, it was far more dangerous to feed some of the other animals that were once kept here! *LISTEN TO THIS!*

POWER PETS

The Tower was once home to some weird and wonderful wild animals that at the time had never been seen in London before. Most of the animals were gifts from foreign rulers. Well, what *do* you give a monarch who has everything? Yep, that's right – an elephant. Or some lions. Or even a polar bear. For a king or queen, having an interesting "pet" from a far-off land was a way to demonstrate their international power and influence. But keeping animals at the Tower in what became known as the Royal Menagerie was often a dangerous business – and not just for the visitors.

A menagerie is the name given to a collection of wild animals kept in captivity.

ZOOLOGY

The first English monarch thought to have had a "zoo" was Henry I (1100–1135). He let lions, leopards, lynxes, porcupines and other exotic beasts roam free on his estate near Woodstock, in Oxfordshire. Luckily there were walls to keep the animals in and the local villagers out!

His descendant Henry III (1216–1272) thought he could improve on the old king's zoo. Why keep these impressive animals hidden away, when you could have them somewhere everyone could see, hear and SMELL them – at the Tower of London? Henry III started the Royal Menagerie with three lions, which were a gift to the king from his brother-in-law. The three big cats were a perfect match for the trio of lions on Henry's coat of arms.

The lion has been a symbol of England and on the coat of arms of kings since at least the eleventh century. Richard I (1189–1199), who was known as Richard the Lionheart, added two more golden lions to the design during his reign.

BEAR NECESSITIES

Henry III was also given a magnificent white bear –
presumably a polar bear – from Norway in 1252. Although it
was kept muzzled and chained, the bear was allowed to swim
and hunt for fish in the Thames, as it was cheaper for it to
catch its own food. A "stout cord" was tied to the bear to keep
it from escaping and its keeper was meant to accompany it on
its fishing trips.

ELEPHANT IN THE ROOM

The polar bear was luckier than the African elephant that
arrived at the Tower in 1255 – a gift to Henry III from Louis IX
of France. The creature was crammed into a tiny room which
was just over 12 metres long and 6 metres wide. As word

got out, huge crowds flocked to the Tower to see the elephant. A monk called Matthew Paris described the elephant as being about ten years old, 3 metres high, with a rough hide and small eyes at the top of his head. He couldn't believe that it ate and drank using its trunk. We're not quite sure what the elephant was given to eat or drink, but my great-uncle Bert always said that it drank beer instead of water. This can't have been good for it – it died within two years, and was buried at the Tower.

The animals' diets didn't get much better. In 1781, one of a pair of ostriches swallowed a large nail that "stopt its passage". Visitors were under the impression that ostriches could digest iron, and thought they were giving it treats by feeding it nails.

TRUNK AGAIN!

In the wild, elephants can live for up to seventy years.

BEER

LION-HEARTED

The lions at the Tower remained everyone's favourites. Successive kings and queens added more of the majestic cats to the menagerie. Many of those lions lived long lives and started breeding in captivity. By the time Edward II (1307–1327) was on the throne, there was an official Keeper of the King's Lions, who earned a regular wage (a bit like our Ravenmaster).

The original menagerie was located in what was known as the Lion Tower by the Western Gate – you walk right over the remains of it when you enter the Tower today. Just imagine that you once would have seen real lions pacing up and down. According to great-uncle Bert, the lions' roaring was so loud it could be heard by people who lived nearby.

ROOOAR!

From Tudor times onwards, the menagerie was a popular attraction for people visiting London. But the animals didn't enjoy anything close to our luxurious living standards. We know their cages weren't cleaned out that often because in 1670, workmen digging foundations near the Lion Tower discovered a quantity of "Stincking Garbage and Offall" that had to be buried again in the night "in a hole digged elsewhere". Whiffy, or what!

> Today the ravens' cages are cleaned out once a week.

BIG CAT-ASTROPHE

The Ravenmaster trusts us (well, maybe not Munin) to roam around the Tower and not steal *too* many of your sandwiches. But did you know that once lion cubs were allowed to walk around freely and could even be petted by the visitors? Unsurprisingly, tragedy struck. In 1686, a "young maid from Norfolk", Mary Jenkinson, was badly attacked when she tried to stroke an adult lion she had played with as a cub. She died the next day, after a botched operation on her injured arm.

In 1698, a writer called Ned Ward visited the Royal Menagerie. He described the various creatures for his readers, including "two pretty-looking hell-cats" that could have "killed at a distance with their very looks". There was also a leopard "that loves not to be looked at". Visitors shouldn't get too close, he wrote, because the leopard was apt to suddenly let fly with a "stream of hot piss", which "stinks worse than a polecat's"!

The big cats were given names. There were a family of lions: Marco, Phillis and their son Nero; two lionesses called Jenny and Nanny; a panther also called Jenny; and three tigers called Will and Phillis, and their son Dick.

STOP MONKEYING AROUND!

MONKEY BUSINESS

It wasn't just the cats that caused chaos. There was a big, very cross baboon that had been brought to the Tower having already killed a cabin boy on its sea journey from Africa. It was known to throw heavy objects at anyone passing by. There was also a very badly behaved "School of Monkeys". Visitors were allowed into their cage, until one of the monkeys "tore a boy's leg".

KEEPING ORDER

The legendary zookeeper Alfred Cops took over in 1822. He loved collecting animals and soon there were over 280 creatures, including more than a hundred rattlesnakes, in the Royal Menagerie.

Things improved … slightly. Mr Cops' zebra was exercised regularly – by being ridden around the Tower by a young boy, and then rewarded with a glass of ale from the canteen (the boy not the zebra).

Cages were made more secure, but accidents still happened. In 1828, a feather-brained secretary bird stuck its long neck into the hyena den and was "deprived of its head in one bite". And Mr Cops was nearly dinner for a hungry boa constrictor after becoming entangled in its deadly coils.

Less fortunate was a young keeper, Joseph Croney, who failed to shut a cage door properly and was pounced on by a leopard. His screams brought other keepers running – and my great-uncle Bert. According to his story, Bert dived at the leopard, trying to distract it, but lost half his tail feathers when the cat swiped at him. Eventually one of the keepers hit the leopard over the head with the butt of a rifle, knocking the leopard unconscious and breaking the gun.

The young keeper was badly injured but survived. My great-uncle was unharmed, but for ever more known as "Baldy Bert".

TELL US ANOTHER STORY, BALDY BERT!

In the most infamous incident, two tigers were let into a lion's cage by mistake, and the three animals immediately were at each other's throats. The fight lasted half an hour, until keepers with heated rods managed to prise the animals apart. The poor lion died of its wounds a few days later.

A NEW ZOO

By the 1830s, people at the Tower were beginning to tire of the danger and the smell and there were concerns about the animals' welfare. In August that year *The Times* announced that around 150 of the "royal beasts" were to be given to the Zoological Society of Great Britain, which had built a splendid new facility in Regent's Park, London. This became the world-famous London Zoo.

Mr Cops stayed on at the Tower, charging half-price admission to see the remaining animals, which included a wolf that escaped and chased a pet dog belonging to a Yeoman Warder. Then in 1835, a monkey badly bit a Tower soldier on the leg. News of the incident reached William IV (1830–1837), who ordered the Duke of Wellington, Constable of the Tower, to shut down the Royal Menagerie for good. Now we're the only creatures that you'll find living at the Tower. And remember, we only bite if you tempt us!

MENAGERIE MADNESS QUIZ

1. What were the first animals kept in the Royal Menagerie?
a) Three lions
b) Three bears
c) Three monkeys
d) Three blind mice

2. Which of these was NOT a name of a lion?
a) Phillis
b) Nero
c) Jenny
d) Wayne

3. Which bird had its head bitten off by a hyena?
a) Secretary bird
b) Receptionist bird
c) Teacher bird
d) Great-Uncle Bert

4. Which famous London animals were inspired by beasts in the Menagerie?
a) Dick Whittington's cat
b) The lions in Trafalgar Square
c) Paddington Bear
d) The white elephant at Elephant and Castle

5. Why did William IV order the Royal Menagerie to be shut in 1835?
a) The animals got too dangerous.
b) The Tower's neighbours complained about the noise.
c) The cages were too small.
d) The keeper was eaten.

CHAPTER EIGHT
MISHAPS AT THE MINT

Find out how and why money was made at the Tower.

Now, who better than Harris to tell a few tales of poisoning and pilfering at the Mint. Harris is hardly a cockney sparrow, but he and his family are East Enders hatched, matched and dispatched all within the sound of the Bow Bells.

All right, my little saucepan lids? 'Arris here to fill you in about some rum goings-on at the Mint, where for hundreds of years, metal was melted into coins.

Just don't ask Harris too many questions about his past; he comes from a right nest of villains!

OI, GROG! Get off my case and go suck on a crisp. It was dangerous work for the men who made the coins, so you can't blame 'em for being tempted to steal a bob or two!

SOLO MINT

A mint is a place where money is made. Metal is melted down and stamped, making the coins that you humans use every day to buy things like Grog's favourite crisps. The Mint was based here at the Tower from the thirteenth century right up until 1812.

There used to be many mints making money all over the country, but in 1279 Edward I (1272–1307) decided it was safer to move the biggest mint to London, into the Tower, where it would be protected by the thick walls. In those days, coins were made from real gold and silver, and working in the Mint was hot, sweaty and dangerous. And what did all that lovely dosh attract? Some very determined thieves.

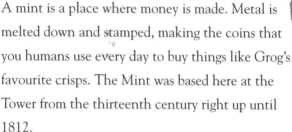

I'M MINTED!

GOLD FINGER

In 1489, the largest coin in England was minted at the Tower. It was 4 cm across, with an image of Henry VII holding the orb and sceptre on it, which is why it became known as a sovereign.

The Mint was hot and noisy, with great fiery furnaces used to melt down the precious metals. The air was full of deadly chemicals and poisonous gases. You wouldn't get me in that building – not for love nor money!

Machinery wasn't used in the Mint until the seventeenth century. So for almost 400 years before that, coins were all made by hand, just as they had been in Roman times.

Making coins was a dangerous business. One man would place a handmade piece of metal between two engraved stamps, then a second man struck it with a hammer. The force of the blow imprinted the marks of the stamp on the metal, creating the coin. But if you took your eyes off the job – ouch! – it was your hand that got flattened, not the coin. Few workers escaped uninjured and the loss of fingers or eyes was common. It was even said that you could spot workers at the Mint by the number of fingers they were missing.

SLEEPING BEAUTY

And losing a finger wasn't the only danger at the Mint. Some nasty chemicals were needed to create coins. William Foxley, a potter at the Mint in the 1540s, one day just fell asleep – and he stayed asleep for fourteen days and fifteen nights. No one could wake him, not even Henry VIII (1509–1547) himself, who, it is said, came to poke the sleeping beauty and couldn't believe his eyes. It could be that the arsenic and lead chemicals used in coin production got to Foxley, but whatever the cause, he woke up perfectly well and continued to live and work at the Tower for another forty years until 1587.

SKULDUGGERY

Less fortunate than Foxley were a group of Germans who worked at the Mint in 1560. They had been hired to make new silver coins for Elizabeth I (1558–1603). One day several men suddenly fell badly ill. It's possible they were poisoned by the noxious gas created by melting the metal. Old hands at the Mint advised the sick men to drink milk as a cure – but it had to be from a human skull! Skulls of the traitors stuck on spikes on London Bridge were nabbed for the job. Despite taking the cure, most of the men died.

HEADS UP!

TROUBLE AND STRIFE

So perhaps it was no surprise that given the job's danger, some workers at the Mint couldn't resist slipping a few newly pressed coins down their breeches. Way back in the 1390s, guess who was one of the first people to try and steal some? The *wife* of the deputy Master of the Mint!

This naughty woman called Joan had fallen for another man, known as John of Ipswich. So she pinched jewels and gold bars from the Mint and ran away. It didn't take a genius to work out where she was headed, and she was arrested in Maldon, Essex, probably on her way to John's home town. Her poor heartbroken husband found himself under suspicion. However, he talked himself out of trouble, ending up as Master of the Mint in 1395! Not even Colonel Sopper can find out in his dusty books what happened to Joan or John, but it probably wasn't pretty.

HIGH STAKES

Creating fake money is called counterfeiting and it could get you into BIG trouble. Messing with the image of the monarch, even on a coin, was considered treason. As punishment, counterfeiters first had their right hands chopped off, along with their man-bits. You don't want those traitors having traitor fledglings, right? And if that wasn't bad enough, in later years the punishment was death: hanging, drawing and quartering for the gents and burning at the stake for the ladies, right up until the eighteenth century. Can you believe it?

But still the lure of making a fortune from fake coins tempted many. Young Catherine Heyland was accused of counterfeiting in 1788, along with an accomplice, Christian Murphy. Although Christian gallantly protested her innocence, an official from the Mint confirmed that equipment discovered

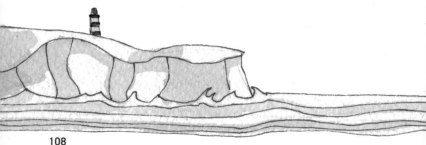

in their room could be used for
counterfeiting. Both were found guilty
and sentenced to death: Christian to
be hanged, and Catherine to be burnt
at the stake.

Newgate Prison was
one of the worst
prisons in London.

Catherine was sent to Newgate Prison and crammed into
a filthy cell with 150 other women to await her fate. In the
nick of time, her execution was delayed by a campaign against
capital punishment. Catherine was saved from the stake, but
transported to Australia on one of the infamous convict ships.

DAYLIGHT ROBBERY

The last major theft from the Mint was in 1798 – and the
thieves nearly got away with it. Early one December morning,
James Turnbull, a former soldier, had just finished striking
several thousand guineas. When the hungry workers left for
breakfast, Turnbull and his best mate Dalton
lagged behind. When everyone had gone,
Turnbull drew a pistol on the supervisor and
demanded keys to the money chest. Ignoring
the supervisor's pleas for him to think
again, Turnbull stuffed four bags of
guineas, containing 2,308 coins and
weighing about 19 kilograms, into
his coat pockets.

He escaped from the Tower and
lay low until 5 January 1799, when
he tried to buy passage to France
on a fishing boat from Dover.
Unfortunately for Turnbull, he was
recognized from a wanted poster
and arrested, with a large amount
of cash on his person. At his trial
on 20 February, he was found
guilty of theft with violence,
although he attempted to clear
his friend Dalton, saying he

knew nothing about the theft but had tried to raise the alarm. Turnbull was hanged on 15 May 1799. It's not known what became of Dalton.

FRESH MINT

In 1810, the Mint finally moved out of the Tower to a new building on Tower Hill filled with steam-powered machinery. It was then moved to Wales in the 1960s and according to my Welsh informer, Bran, security has vastly improved.

MISHAPS AT THE MINT QUIZ

1. Mint workers were easily identifiable by their missing:
   a) toes.
   b) fingers.
   c) eyes.
   d) sense of humour.

2. Why was Henry VIII known as "Old Coppernose"?
   a) He drank too much.
   b) He was very hard-nosed about money.
   c) His sense of smell was rubbish.
   d) Coins made in his reign contained cheap copper, which showed through as the silver wore off.

3. The cure for Mint workers poisoned by fumes was said to be:
   a) drinking milk from a human skull.
   b) drinking blood from a headless chicken.
   c) sucking a silver coin.
   d) drinking five tankards of strong beer.

4. Which two of these were the EARLIEST punishments for male counterfeiters?
   a) Having your right hand chopped off
   b) Having your man-bits removed
   c) Being hanged, drawn and quartered
   d) Burning at the stake

5. Who was Master of the Mint from 1699 to his death in 1727?
   a) Colonel Blood
   b) George Holmes
   c) James Turnbull
   d) Isaac Newton

MYTHS AND NONSENSE

Discover more about the ravens and their stories –
and hear from the Ravenmaster himself.

You've heard a lot of our tales about life at the Tower
over the centuries. The stories may not be the ones in the
official history books, but they are all true. There are also
some rumours about happenings at the Tower that stray
a little further from fact. I've asked my gang for some of
their favourites. **CAN YOU GUESS WHICH
OF THESE STORIES ARE TRUE AND
WHICH ARE FALSE?**

There is a toilet in the upper chamber of the Bell Tower that was installed ready for Adolf Hitler to use if he'd been captured and imprisoned at the Tower during World War II.

SPECIAL SCRATCHY WARTIME ISSUE

Sir Walter Ralegh, imprisoned by James I (1603–1625), was one of the Tower's most famous (and popular) prisoners. He was kept in a comfortable suite of rooms with a garden, in which he grew tobacco plants. He was also encouraged to climb on top of his garden wall and wave at visitors to the Tower to reassure people that he was still alive.

Anne Boleyn, one of Henry VIII's (1509–1547) wives, was brought to the Tower from Greenwich before her coronation in a boat that had a dragon on the prow – that breathed real fire.

The famous diarist Samuel Pepys and his friend, the first Earl of Sandwich, once held several midnight digs at the Tower in 1662, in an unsuccessful attempt to find treasure said to have been hidden by Sir John Barkstead, a former wealthy Tower governor.

There is a secret tunnel underneath the Jewel House so that, in an emergency, the Yeoman Warders can remove the Crown Jewels and take them to safety.

Women used to queue to stick pins into the huge codpiece – a pouch that covered, *ahem*, men's private parts – of Henry VIII's suit of armour. They believed that doing so would help them get pregnant.

OPEN WIDE!

The Beefeaters once had to taste the king's food for poison.

ANSWERS

Harris: FALSE (But Rudolph Hess, one of Hitler's right-hand men, was briefly held at the Tower.)

Munin: TRUE

Gripp: TRUE

Hector: TRUE (Pepys writes about the treasure hunts in his diaries. But no one quite knows about the treasure itself, and we haven't spotted any Yeoman Warders carrying spades around recently.)

Cora: FALSE

Munin: TRUE

Grog: FALSE

A FINAL WORD FROM THE RAVENMASTER

Hello! It's the Ravenmaster here. Now, Grog – that's enough!
I've been listening to all your stories and until now, you've
all stuck to the facts. But this is going too far. A secret tunnel
under the Jewel House, whatever next!

But that doesn't mean we don't all love a legend – like the one about the ravens themselves – and these pesky birds know it. I've heard Grog's story about his Roman ancestors many times, and I think it's now time for me to set the record straight about one or two smaller points in the ravens' history.

Edgar Allan Poe's bestselling poem "The Raven" was published in 1845. The Tower ravens became even more popular after that.

While there have been ravens at the Tower of London for centuries, they were wild birds. They lived alongside us Londoners, helping to keep the medieval streets clean by scavenging for scraps. But these magnificent birds weren't always popular. Some people thought they were a threat to farmers' animals and they were hunted so much that their numbers fell dramatically.

It's most likely that ravens were first kept in captivity at the Tower in the nineteenth century (NOT during Roman times, Grog). The Victorians were fascinated by death and it's well known that Queen Victoria (1837–1901) spent the rest of her life mourning her husband, Albert, when he died aged forty-two. The Victorians were also fascinated by the supernatural. With their dark, mysterious image, the ravens brought a touch of spookiness to the Tower's atmosphere.

NEVERMORE!

119

It's also claimed that after World War II, the Prime Minister, Winston Churchill, ordered a new supply of ravens to cheer up the public and show that the famous ravens and the Tower had survived. The ravens have stayed here ever since.

Today the Tower remains a symbol of power, stability and protection – as well as being a top visitor attraction. And every fortress needs its legends, and we Yeoman Warders love our ravens, even if you take every myth about them with a pinch of salt! In fact, ravens really hate salt. They love a nice crisp, but they wash them first in their water bowls. I've seen them do it!

My job is to make sure that our six ravens – plus one spare – are well looked after. The Tower ravens are bred in Somerset and Wales, and they live here very happily indeed. So to finish off, here are a few TRUE tales about our ravens, straight from me, the Ravenmaster, himself!

DON'T LISTEN TO A WORD HE SAYS!

✱ Ravens are scavengers and are very happy eating rotten meat, but our Tower ravens are fed a diet of fresh meat that I collect from London's famous Smithfield meat market. As a treat, I also give them "specialist meats", like a nice dead rat, day-old chicks or a rabbit.

LOVE RAT!

✱ Ravens can fly, but I make sure they don't fly away. (I don't want to risk the Tower and the kingdom falling!) So just in case, I regularly trim one or two of their flight feathers on one wing, so they become unbalanced and can't fly in a straight line. This doesn't hurt, but it stops them from straying too far. That – and a lot of tasty food, comfortable cages and a huge amount of love from me.

✱ Each raven has a coloured band on one leg to allow visitors to identify them (see the colours by their cages). Ravens in the wild can live a long time – typically ten to fifteen years. Here at the Tower, they can live for even longer. Our oldest raven, James, reached a grand old age of forty-four! Ravens are buried, with full military honours, in a special graveyard at the Tower.

* The ravens choose the Ravenmaster. It's an official role for one of the Yeoman Warders, but you can't be a Ravenmaster if the birds don't like you – and they are quick to spot fear.

* I wear the same uniforms as the rest of the Yeoman Warders, except I have a badge of office on the sleeve of my uniform that depicts the raven head of Bran the Blessed (a Celtic god associated with ravens), the crown (representing the monarch) and a laurel wreath (symbolizing authority – not that the ravens pay much attention to that!).

* The ravens are treated like soldiers at the Tower. If they ever go missing (Munin, I'm looking at you!), they are said to have gone AWOL (a military term that means Absent Without Leave).

* Ravens are brilliant mimics and keep me on my toes by making sounds like car engines, washing machines (remember, they live near the Yeoman Warders' houses) and other birds. One raven called Thor used to say "good morning" to everyone as they passed by.

ATTENTION!

* They are also extremely intelligent and are able to solve problems. They play with each other, sliding down snowy banks in winter and stealing shiny things to impress the other ravens.

* Some ravens do actually play dead, like Gripp, rolling onto their backs and sticking their legs in the air, staying still until I approach. We're not really sure why they do this – to confuse predators in the wild, perhaps. (Or maybe just for a joke!)

* Some ravens are so naughty that they are not allowed to stay at the Tower. A raven called George had to be dismissed for attacking and destroying television aerials. He was issued with a formal SNLR (Services No Longer Required) notice, just like any member of Tower staff or a soldier, and returned to his place of origin.

So now you know what's true and what's just one of Grog's stories! Do come and say hello to us at the Tower. Just remember to keep your crisps hidden at all times!

OI, GEORGE! I WAS WATCHING BRITAIN'S GOT TALONS!

QUIZ ANSWERS

1. HEADS OFF
(p. 30)

1. *b*
2. *c*
3. *d*
4. *b*
5. *c*

2. CROWN JEWELS CALAMITIES
(p. 46)

1. *c*
2. *b*
3. *b*
4. *c*
5. *a, d*

3. A RUFF LIFE
(p. 60)

1. *c*
2. *c*
3. *d*
4. *b*
5. *d*

4. ATTACK AND DEFENCE
(p. 70)

1. *b*
2. *c*
3. *c*
4. *b*
5. *c*

5. GREAT ESCAPES
(p. 80)

1. a, b
2. d
3. a
4. c
5. b

6. COSTUME DRAMAS
(p. 90)

1. c, d
2. c
3. a, b
4. c
5. d

7. MENAGERIE MADNESS
(p. 102)

1. a
2. d
3. a
4. b
5. a

8. MISHAPS AT THE MINT
(p. 112)

1. b, c
2. d
3. a
4. a, b
5. d

ACKNOWLEDGEMENTS

The author would like to thank the creative team
at Walker Books for keeping all feathers unruffled
throughout. Thanks to Ravenmaster Chris Scaife
for his expert input and advice, to Clare Murphy for
adding brilliant jokes, and to Mark Osborne from
Historic Royal Palaces who helped hatch the original
idea. And a big thank you to the ravens for telling their
terrible tales – go see them yourselves at
the Tower of London!

HISTORIC ROYAL PALACES

Historic Royal Palaces is the independent charity that looks after six remarkable palaces: the Tower of London, Hampton Court Palace, Banqueting House, Kensington Palace, Kew Palace and Hillsborough Castle, in Northern Ireland. We raise all our own funds and depend on the support of our visitors, members, donors, sponsors and volunteers. The proceeds from our sales of *Terrible, True Tales from the Tower of London*, and from our gifts and merchandise, go to supporting our work (and keeping the ravens supplied with crisps!). So thank you for buying this book and helping to maintain the beautiful historic buildings for future generations to enjoy.